Animals with Superpowers

Teaching Tips

Turquoise Level 7
This book focuses on the graphemes /u/ ow/.

Before Reading
- Discuss the title. Ask readers what they think the book will be about. Have them support their answer.
- Ask readers to sort the words on page 3. Read the words together.

Read the Book
- Encourage readers to read independently, either aloud or silently to themselves.
- Prompt readers to break down unfamiliar words into units of sound and string the sounds together to form the words. Then, ask them to look for context clues to see if they can figure out what these words mean. Discuss new vocabulary to confirm meaning.
- Urge readers to point out when the focused phonics graphemes appear in the text.

After Reading
- Ask readers comprehension questions about the book. What animals and animal superpowers did they learn about?
- Encourage readers to think of other words with /u/ or /ow/ graphemes. On a separate sheet of paper, have them write the words.

© 2024 Booklife Publishing
This edition is published by arrangement with Booklife Publishing.

North American adaptations © 2024 Jump!
5357 Penn Avenue South
Minneapolis, MN 55419
www.jumplibrary.com

Library of Congress Cataloging-in-Publication Data is available at www.loc.gov or upon request from the publisher.

ISBN: 979-8-88524-766-5 (hardcover)
ISBN: 979-8-88524-767-2 (paperback)
ISBN: 979-8-88524-768-9 (ebook)

Decodables by Jump! are published by Jump! Library.
All rights reserved. No part of this book may be reproduced in any form without written permission from the publisher.

Photo Credits
Images are courtesy of Shutterstock.com. With thanks to Getty Images, Thinkstock Photo and iStockphoto. Cover – Shutterstock. p4–5 –Rawpixel.com, IrinaK. p6–7 - Miguel Scmitter, Maud de Vries. p8–9 – milatas, Greg Amptman. p10–11 – 384, petrdd. p12–13 – Geoffrey Kuchera, MyImages - Micha. p14–15 – alberto clemares exposito. p16 – Shutterstock.

Can you sort these words into two groups? One group has ow as in **now**. One group has ow as in **blow**.

Cow

Glow

Town

Snow

Down

Show

Power

Grown

Do you want to have a superpower? Do you want to glow in the dark? What about rapid speed? Those are both cool powers!

What power do you want?

Superpowers might not be real for humans, but some animals can do things that are just like having superpowers! Some can see in the dark, and some can regrow parts of their bodies.

Some animals can see in the dark. The leaf-tailed gecko can see much better at night than humans can.

How well can you see in the dark?

Cats' pupils are slit shapes. When there is low light, cats' pupils grow wide to let in more light. This helps them see in the dark!

Pupil

Some animals have the power to regrow their different parts. Humans can grow back nails and hair but not an arm or a leg.

When a shark's teeth come out, it is not a problem. Sharks have rows of teeth that can regrow. They can regrow around 30,000 teeth in a lifetime.

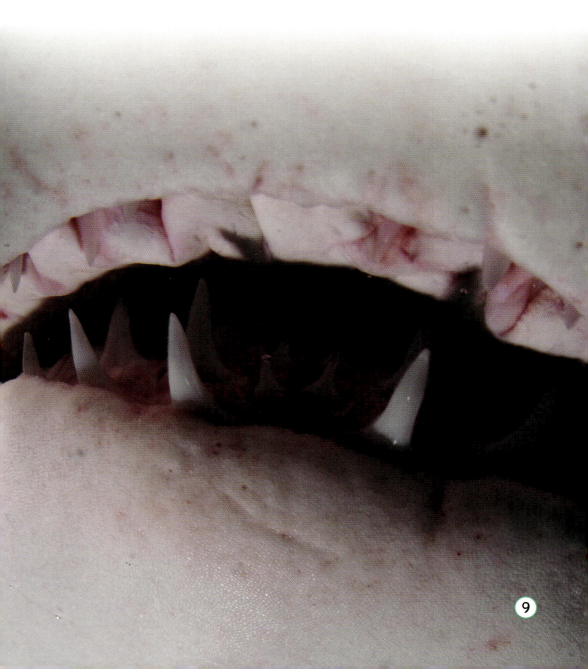

Starfish can have lots of arms. If a starfish loses some of its arms, it can grow them back.

This starfish will grow the missing arm back.

Some animals have the power to make it seem like they have disappeared. The bottom side of the glass frog is clear. This means it can blend in with whatever it sits on.

Lots of animals use their bodies to protect themselves. The skunk has a clever way to do this, but it comes with an awful smell.

Skunks have a gland. They lift up their tail to an attacker, show the gland, and then spray an awful-smelling liquid on them!

Some animals attack other animals. Bulls have big horns. They can attack different bulls to show them how powerful they are.

If you had a superpower, what might it be? Can you draw it? You might have horns like a bull or pupils to see in low light like a cat!

Say the name of each object below. Is the "ow" in each an /ow/ sound or a long /o/ sound?

cow

bow

crow

clown